PASSPORTS, PURSES, AND PLANES!

Jennifer,
Thank you for
supporting me!
Eugenia

First Step to Solo Travel for
the Woman Over 50

EUGENIA VIGIL

Passports, Purses, and Planes!
First Steps to Solo Travel for the Woman Over 50
Published by Contessa Press
Castle Rock, CO

ISBN: 978-0-578-53409-1

TRAVEL / Special Interest / Senior

Cover and interior design by Victoria Wolf

QUANTITY PURCHASES: Companies, professional groups, clubs, and other organizations may qualify for special terms when ordering quantities of this title. For information, email contessa.pub@gmail.com.

CONTENTS

Introduction

HISTORY. That provocative, ever-changing, some-times repetitive noun, which stirs up inquisitiveness that leads to bravery, anger, protests, praise, and laughter.

History intrigues me. I sought investigation into Bartolome Esteban Murillo, a Spanish Baroque painter from the mid-seventeenth century. His passion, expressed in his paintings, came through the people of Seville, Spain (the poor, the prostitute, children of the street, and the faithful). I sought to see that passion in person: Bartolome Murrillos's paintings and the place that inspired him.

I pursued answers for most of my life, seeing and touching the creativity of those in history who created or stood centuries ago and being able to touch the "tip of the earth." History guided me to Spain, where I followed the steps of my beloved Spanish artist and visited the cathedrals where the faithful commissioned and hung Bartolome's majestic paintings.

Over the past thirty-five years, I have visited Scotland, Paris, Spain, Germany, London, and numerous cities and towns throughout Canada, Mexico, and the United States. Alone or with my family, I have experienced history, gained confidence, and worked out difficult situations—or allowed them to work out!

I wrote this book to encourage, educate, warn, and to prepare other travelers, specifically women over forty-five years of age who travel as solo passengers, not to boast about my travels or show slides or to pull out the family scrapbook. Traveling to the sites you have always wanted to visit and seeing them at your own pace feels extremely rewarding.

As you proceed past this page, you will find practically all of the guidance needed to arrange a travel experience worth remembering. I meticulously researched every step, from that first travel concept to discovering how to get across the town you wish to visit. (For example, a train or a taxi.)

My observations and conversations with other colleagues make me suggest you keep your first excursion local, say to the nearest city or within 100 miles. Take notes. Find out what's most important to you such as the residence you booked or how you planned entertainment around transportation and timing issues. Venture out to a restaurant or a movie; take a taxi or rent a car. No one attempts to climb Mount Everest without careful planning, strength, and mental training over time. I'm using the comparison to train you, like an athlete, and to provide an intellectual perspective and a proven method.

Also, this handbook is meant to fold into your back pocket as you travel, to tear out the pages needed, or to write out the hotels, airlines, and other arrangements onto the book's pages.

Congratulations on making a first step if you haven't solo journeyed before. If you will embark on a different mode of travel, please enjoy this successful compilation of travel data that I have meticulously penned over thirty-five years of travel and put together for you! Enjoy it to the fullest!

I'm honored that you chose to begin your travel by reading my handbook!

Bon voyage!

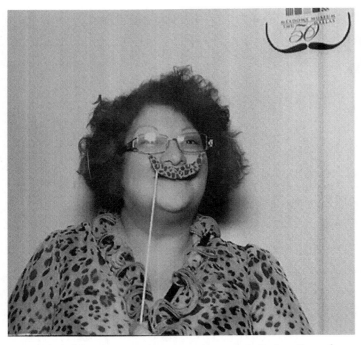

At a gala held at the SMU Meadows Museum in Dallas, Texas for a new acquisition of a Salvador Dali painting.

Obtaining a Passport

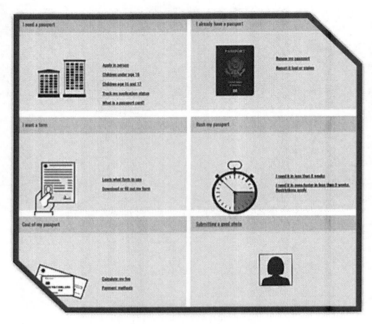

Photo courtesy of The U.S. Department of State website, travel.state.gov/content/travel/en/passports.html/passport_1738.html

* Before any travel plans come to fruition, plan to visit your local licensing office or access the following website to obtain documents to process your passport (www.travel.state.gov/content/travel/en/passports.html/). A passport is not only used for travel but serves as an extra, valid identification source.

* There are two options for receiving information when obtaining a passport. Whether you are renewing or ordering a new passport, you MUST request it four to six weeks in advance of your departure date if traveling outside your country. It takes that amount of time to process the forms and to seek clarification if needed. In the past, I've overheard many applicants become frustrated (sometimes enraged!) because they were told they couldn't receive it in a single day (unless it was classified as a life-or-death situation). You WILL pay a hefty amount in expedited fees for a two or three week delivery of your passport.

* Submit a photo with the documents. Follow the specific guidelines detailed on the website or the office will NOT approve your application.

* In some instances, you might need to replace your passport while overseas or across borders.

There are several pointers I can pass along that you must apply for an effortless trip. First, contact the embassies of the countries you will be visiting and provide the necessary documentation they need. (There is possibly a website for that embassy; make sure it is the valid governmental website.) Second, make two color copies of the first two pages of your passport that include a picture ID and your personal information. Personally, I include a copy in a folder with all the information about my trip. (Please see the following section giving information on creating a folder.) Give the other copy to a trusted individual who could fax it to you in case of an emergency. Also, I would make a copy of birth certificates. I would include a baptismal record, if available, because there are countries that uphold the Catholic religion and use that document as a valid type of identification.

My Experience

As my family and I entered an Eastern European country through customs, a certain agent who checked our credentials decided to test my nerves. He asked where we were staying, for how many days, the names of the customer service (CS) agent at the hotels, the telephone numbers of every location we planned to visit, what time we would leave the hotel to arrive at the airport, and the restaurants where we planned to eat. (Unbelievable, right?). Some questions were, of course, justified. I am eternally grateful that I was blessed with the knowledge to have made an incredible folder of our detailed vacation in advance. He simply brushed me forward with my passport in hand. (Please see the section on creating a folder of documents for your travel.)

Once you have obtained the passport, you are definitely ready for your adventure!

CHECKLIST

✓ Prepare a month or two in advance of your trip.

✓ Log onto the US Department of State website (under the RESOURCES tab) and research the photo specifications required for the passport.

✓ Locate the nearest facility that can take a passport photo. Many mailing and pharmacy convenience stores offer passport services, including CVS Pharmacy, Walgreens, Walmart, some UPS stores (some are individually owned), and FedEx stores. (Call before you visit.) You can also visit the AAA website and select SEARCH, then type in PASSPORT for a list of AAA passport photo stores (www.aaa.com/office/).

✓ Validate your documents and your photo on the US Department of State website.

✓ Visit the following website to locate the passport agency in your local area. (travel.state.gov/content/travel/en/passports.html/passport_1738.html.) Bring your birth certificate, driver's license, and the photo for processing at your local or state passport agency.

My travel folder showing the cities that I would be travelling to, as a tab and inside were printed hotel confirmations, airline tickets, train maps and entertainment options.

Organizing Planned Dates and Places

NOW THAT YOU HAVE LINED up a proposed city, state, or country for your upcoming travel, read through the following important tips you will need to proceed on your journey. Again, I learned this over thirty-five years of solo and family travel within the US, Canada, the United Kingdom, Mexico, and throughout Europe. Using strong organizational skills and possessing a willingness for change and adventure make these references strong.

* Print out or pull up a full month's calendar of your possible travel period.

* Verify plans or upcoming events with your children, grandparents, and loved ones during that potential travel period.

* Reschedule mail, milk, or any other delivery services or delegate the matters to a neighbor or a friend.

* Do your holidays occur during your travel? Use a search engine to locate holidays occurring in that

prospective country or countries. This step is very important. Many countries such as Spain (where I have traveled on numerous occasions), practice and pilgrimage during many religious holidays. I know of a country that many commoners travel out of their countryside for a vacation that they normally never take during the year.

- Also, certain regions of Spain follow a daily custom called "the siesta." Learn about these cultural practices in advance. Many business establishments close down for a period of one to three hours during the day to rest. No need to worry: many establishments proceed again beginning at seven or eight o'clock in the evening.

✱ Create a timeline for your entire trip.

- Bring out the colored pens or pencils and your drawing tablet (or whatever blank paper you can claim as your own.) Fast food napkins do not work!—You know who you are!

- Draw a horizontal line with tick lines an inch apart. (Each line represents a calendar day— from departure to arrival in your home city.)

- Add in the places surrounding the dates after you've created a rough sketch of the places you have selected to travel. For me, I like seeing this on a daily basis before my trip. I can add events, tours, and visits to relatives or friends and rearrange dates or places easily by seeing an organized planner of dates.

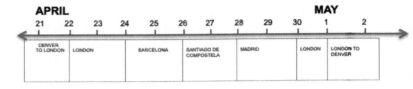

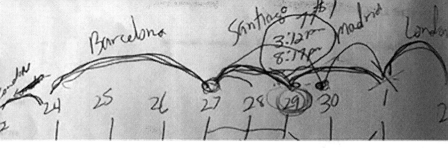

The rough sketch details my departure from Denver, Colorado on April 21st with a full day crossing the ocean (UK time). Then I spent the 22nd through the 24th in London. From the 24th through the 27th, I planned on travelling to Barcelona, Spain. From the 27th through the 29th, I visited Santiago de Compostela, Spain. From April 29th through the 1st of May; a travel stop to Madrid. May 1st through the 2nd became the last tour through London. And on July 2nd, I departed back home to Denver.

CHECKLIST

✓ Know and finalize the weeks or months of your scheduled vacation.

✓ Select a family member, neighbor, or friend as an emergency contact. Give them a hard copy of your passport and the name of the residence(s) where you will be staying (both addresses and phone numbers).

✓ Arrange for someone to pick up your mail.

✓ Research the states, countries, villages, or other locations you plan to visit to avoid site-wide conventions that may block your ability to book a room.

✓ Sketch or create a timeline of your entire trip in a notebook or on a graphic design or spreadsheet app.

✓ If you are traveling out of the US, research celebrations and major holidays to choose whether or not you wish to join in on the festivities. (Examples: Running of the Bulls or Ramadan.)

✓ Make a list of your monthly bills, including due dates and amounts.

TOOLKIT

✓ A two-pocket folder with three-hole punch fasteners, including plastic tab sheets or colored papers to separate your travel items. (Include airports you will arrive and depart from, air flight numbers, places you'll stay, and entertainment.)

✓ A printed calendar covering the dates of your trip.

RESOURCES

✓ Use a calendar and organization app on your cell phone or computer, or an app purchased on your app store. You can list when and where your travel will originate.

✓ Some suggestions include Cozi, Google Calendar, iCloud for Mac, Microsoft Outlook, Fantastical 2 for the iPhone, CloudCal for Android, and Jorte Calendar for Windows.

✓ There are many others. Please check to see if they are compatible with your cell phone.

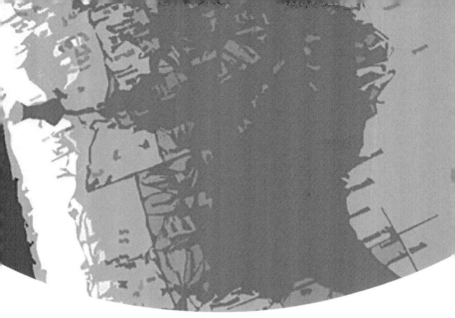

Pin several areas where you might want to travel to

Travel Within the United States

THERE IS MORE RED TAPE accompanying international travel (though these experiences are worth every paper, penny, and immunization shot!), but local travel also requires detailed organization.

Any kind of travel essentially requires researching motels, hotels, bed and breakfasts, rented homes or condos, hostels, or other options. Popular hotel websites list various types of residences (a few sites I selected and listed under RESOURCES in this section). Historical or modern art may be a draw to your eye, including architecture—from the outside to the inside foyer and the rooms. Personally, I like a certain brand of hotel chain that includes all the amenities I like. I list them under my profile when I book a room.

I listed important points to consider as you research a place of residence.

Do you want to be situated near:

* Trendy gathering spots such as downtown or more touristy areas
* Several local restaurants
* Certain types of transportation (bus, train, rail, or a taxicab drop-offs)
* Paths to walk during the night or day
* The airport

* Gas stations
* Parking (consider pricing and safety)
* Major highways or streets
* Family or friends
* Pet-friendly residences
* Scenery
* Great fishing spots
* Major shopping areas
* Tour bus entry points
* Hot springs pools
* Winery stops

OTHER OPTIONS TO CONSIDER ABOUT TYPES OF RESIDENCES

* A restaurant within the residence
* A pool, hot tub, sauna, or workout facility
* Breakfast
* A bathtub
* Guest shops
* A spa
* Specific resort features
* Workout facilities

* Free shuttles in the vicinity or to the airport
* Concierge services
* Free wi-fi
* A business center
* A coffee shop
* A refrigerator or microwave
* A safe for valuables
* Comfortable foyer settings
* Camping locations
* Scenic views
* Age-appropriate accommodations
* Updated furniture and room features
* Being in a safe neighborhood
* Close transportation options
* Reliable recommendations from friends, family, or a residence's reference website for hotels, motels, bed and breakfasts, rented houses, or condos

CONSIDERATIONS FOR CRUISES

* A view of the water
* Proximity to an elevator

* Avoiding families with children
* Various entertainment options aboard
* Musical performances
* The islands, cities, or docking places
* Age-appropriate tour groups
* Kitchen nooks, bathtubs, or living room options

RENTING A VEHICLE

I recommend renting a vehicle if you are embarking on a road trip. Take into consideration the resistance of road testing your new vehicle or economizing by using your own vehicle as well. Some rental car companies offer very inexpensive deals and will advertise specials at the beginning of the week.

They offer options to purchase their insurance or you could investigate your own personal liability or collision insurance. The choice is yours. However, I usually take their offered insurance. It covers unusual damage like hail, rock damage, or deer collisions. The automobile may require repairs that you didn't know existed upon contract. Again, read their contract or check with your personal insurance carrier.

CHECKLIST

✓ Evaluate several different residence options, airlines, and entertainment based on your specifications or my sample list from above.

✓ Contact CS concerning if the pool is being serviced.

✓ Check if construction issues or major conventions will impact your week, including road construction, updating the interiors of your residence, or issues with transportation options getting to your destination.

✓ Take notes about everything you want to do and the places you want to see!

✓ Attend a one- to two-day course given by a tour group, cruise agency, or a featured speaker. Using AAA services is essential for me because I get twenty-four-hour mobile phone care when I travel, extensive and exclusive deals only for members, printed travel guides for all parts of the world for purchase at their agency, in-house travel agents to book all types of travel (local or overseas), and the ability to purchase different types of world currencies.

TOOLKIT

✓ A printed road atlas. (I know, so archaic, right?) Study the cities, towns, roads, and major entertainment venues that dot this beautiful land of ours.

✓ Visitor guides for the places you may visit (printed or online).

RESOURCES

✓ Rental car websites for Avis, Enterprise, Hertz, Alamo, Budget, and Payless—to name a few.

✓ Third-party travel websites, including Travelocity, Expedia, Trivago, and Kayak, and others that track airline discount prices such as Hopper and Priceline.

✓ Major airlines such as Frontier, Southwest, American, Alaska, United, and Delta. When booking a hotel and car with a flight, agencies will usually offer a major discount for buying together. Compare prices if this is important to you.

✓ Begin accruing airline miles with a certain airline or a third-party website; this is a good beginning. I have certain airline miles with a direct airline, and it sometimes is beneficial. You may purchase a credit card to earn additional miles, but I don't recommend doing so unless it is necessary as a backup or for security purposes. I advise against disclosing your personal banking information when you travel.

As the U.S. is now the largest wine-consuming nation in the world, many states are now creating their own wineries. Along with wineries, distilleries and breweries are now becoming the social norm of our society.

Global Positioning Systems (GPS) vs. Printed Maps

MAPS, AS YOU KNOW, are essential for areas that are not picked up by data coverage and unidentifiable locations (being lost!), searching for that restaurant sworn by the concierge to be the best food in town, or if you forget where the train station entrance is located. I listed several options I have used in the past that are all viable. (Each option serves a different purpose.)

* The GPS attached to your rental car

* A GPS app downloaded on your cell phone

* Printed maps

* Hotel maps

* Vacation brochure maps

* Double-decker hop-on/hop-off visitor maps

* For cruises: upon docking at a port, ask the ship's entertainment director to direct you to shopping and restaurants, which dissuades

their tourists from going out of the approximate boundaries set by them.

★ AAA travel maps, including walking and driving maps, large foldouts of the entire countryside, and small, pocket-size maps of a general area.

★ **GPS devices** are a great choice for navigation. You can purchase a sole navigation system that plugs into a car's USB port. Read the instructions first, and then install it onto your on-board car computer system or onto your cell phone.

★ GPS also comes readily available with all **cell phones**. Check your cell phone network provider to see if they cover the territory you're visiting or what plans can you temporarily add to your phone, text, and GPS navigation. (Some networks allow you to cancel the added international plan when you return home.)

★ Cell phone map apps easily adapt to automobiles' Bluetooth computer modules. Depending on the auto's module, you can often see the map area from your cell phone map app directly on-board. Sometimes the map app will broadcast through the module also.

★ **Hotel maps** provided by your concierge or front desk are significant because they include train or bus terminals and highly visited tourist destinations. The hotel staff will point out and circle places you want to venture out to during the day or week, plus highly recommended restaurants in the vicinity. Since they have been educated on the tourist hotspots, they are usually proficient in showing the best areas to tourists. They also redirect after-hours listings, in case a service entry is closed.

★ With your own **guidebooks or printed maps**, you can write on them or tear out several key areas or tourist finds (only guides that you have purchased, of course!) I usually bring several that I have previously researched and stuff those excerpts into my backpack.

* The **hop-on/hop-off** double-decker tourist buses also offer maps. These maps come complimentary with your bus ticket and are helpful because they include entertainment and cultural venues PLUS where to catch the next line to return to your accommodations. But keep in mind, those buses have a start and stop time.

MY EXPERIENCE

During a trip in Hamburg, Germany, my family and I decided to purchase a ticket for the hop on/hop off tour bus. However, we did not verify the last stop at the drop-off site for the final bus. As a result, we walked for three hours to get back to the hotel. As a family, we were safe. However, as a solo traveler, I would take precautions and check in advance.

CHECKLIST

✓ Choose an option: a GPS device, a cell phone, computer-generated maps, hotel or travel agency printed maps, or other options.

✓ Your cell phone, in case of an emergency.

✓ Your residence's business card and taxi and police phone numbers.

✓ A variety of maps to access local sights, tourist areas, restaurant locales, and entertainment options.

RESOURCES

✓ Download your cell phone carriers map
  app or go to the STORE app and download a convenient map.

✓ Download entertainment information from
  travel sites like AAA, TripAdvisor, Entertain-
  ment-Plus.net (North America only), and
  Viator.com.

✓ There are many more to choose from.
  Locate your selections on the maps and
  underline them, tab the entries, or call
  customer support for more information.

On the subject of phones ...

The Rosetta Stone, British Museum.

Communication Choices

VERIFY NETWORK SIGNALS and coverage areas before your trip. Purchasing an international plan, chip, or extra phone for communication is helpful. Using your phone helps you find certain locations, and you can contact your residence or purchase a night at a hotel off of the beaten path—and, of course, for any unforeseen emergency that may occur.

Cell phones or Apple iPADs, Amazon Kindles, or Microsoft's Surface GO can be used as a multifunctional resource. Whether it is that late-night game of Fortnight, Candy Crush Saga, or TETRIS®, reading the latest novel you haven't had the time for, or finishing the last report your boss needs by the end of the week, a handheld device can accomplish all of the above tasks and services. (Very important! Remember to download all your apps, including gaming apps, before you leave your home.)

Open up your cellphone app store and peruse their gallery to aid or extend your curiosity. Here are just a few that I tapped into after reading the magazine iPhone Life, Fall 2019. I like these exciting new apps, although there are more. (NOTE: Some only work for US travel and not internationally. Check the description before downloading.)

* Photography, including Adobe Lightroom, Moldiv, and Musemage

* Health and fitness such as WebMD, My Diet Coach, Yoga Studio, 30-Day Fitness Challenge (a walking/step counter), and Strava for running (maps routes, noting your speed, and distance)

* Download your favorite movie or series with Hulu, Hiappo, Vudu, and others

* Use FaceTime, Skype, or Google Duo for live video chatting

* Use Grubhub, Ubereats, or DoorDash for food delivery and takeout

* Wordscapes or solitaire will keep your mind fresh

* Use Calm and Eight Sleep to aid your sleeping patterns

* Access Hulu or Amazon for music, movies, or podcast downloads

* iRosetta Stone, Duolingo, or Google Translate help you when ordering a nice dinner at a restaurant

* Hello Vino pairs wine with what you plan to eat

* Expensify scans receipts to add up your trip expenses

* Watch individually produced videos or past shows you've missed and much more on YouTube

* Napster, TuneIn Radio, or iHeartRadio play your favorite types of music

* BlindSquare, Google, or Apple Maps use real-time GPS data

And so much more! Peruse the entire app gallery; see what may stimulate the mind and your trip! Try similar apps that may be more efficient than the ones I have shared!

Most of Europe and other countries throughout the world use WhatsApp® to communicate for free. Their website explains the main purpose for users, and it is encoded for security

OUR MISSION

"WhatsApp started as an alternative to SMS. Our product now supports sending and receiving a variety of media: text, photos, videos, documents, and location, as well as voice calls. Our messages and calls are secured with end-to-end encryption, meaning that no third party, including WhatsApp, can read or listen to them. Behind every product decision is our desire to let people communicate anywhere in the world without barriers."
www.whatsapp.com/about

OMGoodness! WhatsApp® is so versatile. You could use a wi-fi signal while using this app instead of data, especially if your phone plan offers limited data. Also, some American fast-food giants or cafés offer free wi-fi. Plus, all hotels and motels (and most hostels)

include free wi-fi with your accommodation package. However, take precautions when they require you to download an app to use their free wi-fi.

Again, as stated above in the GPS chapter, US phone networks have international plans that you can enroll in for the month you will travel. Some networks allow you to cancel the added plan as soon as you return home. Some countries provide insertable SIM chips for purchase into your American phone. Your network provider, the internet search engine, or social networking friends who have traveled abroad can give you tips for getting a network signal.

I used the international call plan on top of WhatsApp. Both were very helpful during my trips when I wanted to speak with my family or contact the next hotel on my trip. Of course, in some circumstances, the plan may not reach certain small towns or natural areas. That is where you will need to implement your photographic memory, notes, and compass rules.

If you are visually or physically handicapped and have lost your phone device, call the emergency phone number and US embassy in that country. If at all possible, they will retrieve or find a similar device in extreme cases.

My traveling colleagues and I highly advise that you learn ten words or phrases that can be translated for general purposes. Examples include: "Where is the bathroom?," "Do you have anything on your menu for vegetarians?," "How do I get to _____?," "Where can I find the nearest _____?," "Please," "Thank you," "Hello," "Goodbye," "Where do I catch the _____?" and "How much does this cost?"

These are just a few suggestions. Also, learning hand gestures, physical touches, clothing, kind remarks, and offensive words or other offensive terms should be researched and avoided.

CHECKLIST

✓ Purchase an international plan, chip, or extra phone for communication.

✓ Know international plans exclusions, and research phone chips or if purchasing a phone overseas is more functional.

✓ Peruse your cell phone app store to download apps that will make your adventure more enjoyable!

✓ Obtain a business card from your residence's front desk phone and a taxicab company, in case data doesn't reach out to your destination.

✓ (Very important!) Know your cell phone provider and their telephone number in case your phone becomes lost or stolen, so they can lock or disable it.

✓ Purchase a charge powerstation or other portable charger that will charge your phone in an instant while you are mobile. This is a handy device. It can charge your phone at the end of the day as well.

RESOURCES

✓ Download WhatsApp and all other apps onto your cell phone before leaving the U.S.. It might be difficult to download apps from the airport or another country. Cell phone companies have put up preventive measures because of hacking and stolen identity incidents. Therefore, downloading apps may not install properly or at all.

✓ Read several articles on travel websites such as Trip Advisor or AAA or widely known travel blogs such as www.Rick-Steves.com or www.travel.AARP.org that detail how other travelers communicate by cell phone in particular parts of the country.

✓ Research and Download a Translation app. Such apps include Google Translate, iTranslate, and Waygo. For help with interpreting food menus, look into Microsoft Translator and TripLingo. Some may be specific to a certain language or cell phone brand.

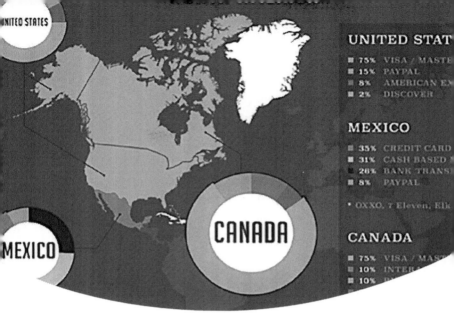

UNITED STAT

- ▪ **75%** VISA / MASTE
- ▪ **15%** PAYPAL
- ▪ **8%** AMERICAN EX
- ▪ **2%** DISCOVER

MEXICO

- ▪ **35%** CREDIT CARD
- ▪ **31%** CASH BASED
- ▪ **26%** BANK TRANS
- ▪ **8%** PAYPAL

• OXXO, 7 Eleven, Elk

CANADA

- ▪ **75%** VISA / MAST
- ▪ **10%** INTER
- ▪ **10%**

*"Online Payment Methods around the World". Published in an
article by Dan Barraclough, expertmarket.co.uk/merchant-accounts.
This graphic is only a sample given from the website, www.adyen.
com/home/business-intelligence/country-payment-guides.html.*

Currency: What, Where, When, and How

Whether traveling in the US or out of the country, research how to reserve cash for your trip.

US TRAVEL

* US currency
* Credit cards
* E-Wallet/digital wallet apps
* A separate debit account
* Currency conversions (how much and why)

Withdraw at least $200 to $300 in US currency for three to four days when you need to purchase more international currency during your travels. If you purchase a substantial amount of foreign currency that doesn't coincide with the number of days you plan to visit that certain country, you will have to exchange it at a lower rate or keep it until you get to an American bank for a reasonable exchange rate.

Divide and store your currency in different areas such as your wallet, waist belt, or other secure places.

Having a **credit card** (from an established bank) is a highly acceptable currency backup. Remember to write down your security pin in a safe place or download an app that safely stores passwords. When purchasing items, hotel and car rentals, or restaurant meals, charges such as unapproved damage deposits, extra fees, or tips will be accessed through the credit card.

A credit card company can trace unauthorized purchases or cancelation issues that may occur. I use my credit card solely for hotel and car rental purchases. You can dispute a purchase, and the credit card company will do the investigation.

An innovative function shaping the way we access our credit and debit accounts, health care, and even a Starbucks account in one location is called the **E-Wallet or a digital wallet**. Many countries accept this form of payment instead of the monetary system used traditionally throughout the world. Several major cell phone operating systems (such as Apple Pay, Samsung Pay, and Android Pay) have incorporated these "wallets" as a more convenient way to purchase goods and services.

Other apps that are specific to a business include Walmart and Starbucks payment apps. Two other forms of financial procurement include Venmo and E-Wallet from Ilium Software. According to the website

Investopedia in their article on "Top 3 Mobile Wallets of 2019" (www.investopedia.com), Venmo is a social commerce app that repays others in their social circle, while an E-Wallet stores your credit cards, account numbers, passwords, and fingerprints like a warehouse. Many different credit cards can be swiped using this particular app.

The most popular E-Wallet, used throughout the world, is Paypal. If you research the websites www.ayden.com or www.expermarket.co.uk, they offer a more precise map of the world and their top payment options. Some include E-Wallets aligned with the country's currency. These options might be a better resource for you because they charge the exact currency rate, and you can verify the amount through your phone. (**Very important!** It is vital to carry currency from that country for taxis and other forms of transportation.)

Banking institutions offer their **banking apps**, which can be downloaded onto your cell phone. You can view your credit account information immediately. However, I advise you NOT to use your bank account if you are traveling abroad.

MY EXPERIENCE

As I waited for my connecting flight home from a well-known US city, I purchased a food item through a kiosk in the airport. Twenty minutes later, my bank's fraud department called and asked me if I had purchased a $200 item three times. I was horrified that this had happened, although these days, you have to protect your bank account at all costs. It is better to use one credit card account, preferably a major brand; that way you can dispute fraudulent charges.

You can access your banking or credit card app through your mobile phone by tapping, a thumbprint, or facial recognition without fumbling through your notebook of usernames and passwords. Some users like to upload their credit card information into a "wallet" feature such as the app that comes with your phone when you purchase it. This feature will protect you in an emergency, in case you misplace or forget your credit card case in your hotel room. Certain dining, clothing, and fast-food establishments have a system on their registers that allows you to tap your cell phone device onto certain credit card teller machines for your E-Wallet app, and it charges it automatically.

INCREMENTS OF INTERNATIONAL CURRENCY

For international currency, I usually carry $100 separated into:

$1–$10
Handy for tips and change for snack machines

$10–$20
Quick purchases or gasoline

$50–$100
Transportation (cabs, trains, or buses)

Foreign currency fluctuates every day, depending on the exchange market.

There are several places to purchase foreign currency. Each of these institutions charge a transaction fee. Some may charge a considerable amount, and calling these institutions is the best way to check the fee rates.

* Major banks (most local banks will not offer this service)
* AAA travel agencies
* Airports (the US or overseas)
* Major malls in the US
* Several outlets along main streets or city squares

(Note: Airports, malls, and outlets in cities or out of the country may have a higher purchase rate for foreign currency. I have listed these last because their charges are under their control of the conversion rate or their transaction fees.)

Major banks know the current value of the currency you wish to purchase. If you are comfortable with the rate, you can purchase it immediately, or you can wait until the end of the week.

AAA travel agencies also offer currency. Call your branch to ensure they have your currency in stock and ask about their transaction rate.

Some, not all, credit or debit card institutions need to charge transaction fees. Contact the CS department of the credit card company listed on the back of your card to check if they charge for this service. Credit cards provide some insurance backup, in case of loss or theft. Let them know the timeline and the places where you will be traveling before your trip. It is very important to communicate with the bank's CS. Otherwise, your card may be placed on hold due to unexpected purchases made hundreds or thousands of miles away from your city.

MY EXPERIENCE

I took a taxicab ride back to my hotel, and the driver spoke very little English. He wanted me to pay with currency. However, I did not have the right change, so I handed him my credit card. With a snarl, he ran my credit card through the credit machine twice. When I reached my hotel room, I had a funny feeling that he charged me twice for the cab ride. I quickly contacted my credit card company through webchat. I asked if a recent transaction ran twice for the same amount. The outcome was not pleasant, although they quickly resolved the issue. Having that assurance made my trip a little easier, knowing my accounts were insured. My major credit card company offers webchat, which is useful, due to being overseas and avoiding a heavy telephone fee (for being on hold or pressing five to seven different automated call routing options).

CHECKLIST

✓ Types of currency to bring along on your trip.
  ✓ Credit or debit cards
  ✓ Foreign currency
  ✓ American money

✓ Carry $100–$200 of American currency in case you need to purchase more foreign currency.

✓ Contact your credit card company's CS department, listed on the back of your card, and your banking institution, and notify them about the countries where you will be vacationing.

✓ Write your credit card security pin down in a safe place or download a secure password app.

✓ Research the most economical places to purchase foreign exchange currency before you travel (a bank, AAA, other travel agency, or public areas like a mall or an airport).

✓ Research the institution you will use for foreign currency two to three weeks before you travel in case the institution needs to preorder it from another location. Contact the institutions first for their transfer rates.

RESOURCES

✓ Download your cell phone E-Wallet feature. Keep all usernames and passwords in secured NOTES or a SAFE app such as Password Padlock-Microsoft Store, 1Password, LastPass, DataVault for Windows, or Dashlane.

✓ Research www.expertmarket.co.uk and www.adyen.com. Locate the map for "Online Payment Methods Around the World" to view the most current methods of payment used throughout the world.

✓ Research your cell phone operating systems apps. The most downloaded are Apple Pay, Venmo (valid only when used in the US), PayPal (most widely used throughout the world), Google Pay, Android Pay, Samsung Pay, and Microsoft's E-Wallet app. View their guidelines and restrictions.

✓ Download an app called XE Converter if not using the particular apps described above. Their website also converts currency: www.xe.com/currencyconverter.

There is nothing like taking a nap on an airplane! Especially when there isn't enough room to spread out. Bring your neck pillow and earplugs and you are set! Shhhh...

Airlines: Lesser-Known vs. Well Established

YOU MIGHT ACHIEVE a speedier output of flight and a lower price by going online instead of using a travel agency. It takes some research to choose flights for your peace of mind and preferences. My spur-of-the-moment bookings are usually sparked by a lower fare. I tend to select other bookings for seat comfort, meals on board, and other preferences. Consider the following when choosing an airline.

AIRLINES

* Lowest fare
* Nonstop or one stop
* Comfort of seating
* Seat space between passengers
* Meals served on board
* Media options (games, movies, and other entertainment options)
* Variety of drinks (alcohol or non-alcoholic)
* Size of the airplane
* Free carry-on or free baggage check
* Airline miles reward
* Reliable CS

RESERVATIONS

There are choices you can make about who will make reservations for you and how they will be made. (The same information applies to "Hotels and Other Residency Options.")

* AAA travel
* Third-party travel metasearch engines such as Expedia, Hotwire, Hotels.com, Travelocity, TripAdvisor, CheapOAir, LastMinuteTravel. com, and many others). **These websites also offer last minute flights**
* Direct airlines (through their websites)
* Travel agencies in your local area
* Yourself or another traveler
* Hotel websites that offer discount packages, including flights, hotels, cars, entertainment, and all-inclusive package deals

Another consideration when booking an airline is the airports. Lines may be long, as they are connected with check-in and receiving luggage. Research the preferred airlines by other people who have flown that particular brand, including how the CS agents handled canceled flights and other situations.

CHECKLIST

✓ Categorize in three columns what you prefer regarding an airline, including the size of the plane, seating, and drinks.

✓ Large airlines offer benefits such as flight rewards. Decide which rewards you prefer and what airline flies to the most cities from your location.

✓ Check if the airline flies to that city more than once a day. In case of weather or any other delay, they may put you on another outbound flight.

✓ Choose between a travel agency, a travel search engine, or a direct airline for booking a reservation.

RESOURCES

✓ Major and minor airline websites that give a definite description of where they fly and specific flight arrival and departure times.

✓ Use Google Flights, a comprehensive flight search engine, to identify prospective costs throughout a given year for a particular region you wish to visit.

✓ Third-party travel metasearch engines such as Expedia, Hotwire, Travelocity, TripAdvisor, and many other sites are useful. However, they only work with major airline websites.

Which leads us to...

Once you have your luggage, ticket, passport (if needed), and small essentials tucked away in your purse or backpack, you are set to enter into your next stage of adventure!

Airports

Plan distance and time and transportation concerning airports. View your itinerary the day before you fly out to your next destination. Make sure you know which airport you will be flying out of on every trip. Don't assume that you will fly out of the same airport that you arrived in. Many larger cities, in the US or overseas, have more than one airport. Some airlines fly out of a different airport than their competitors.

Find the best transportation option that takes you directly to the airport, and make sure the time and distance will be within two to three hours before the departure time.

OPTIONS

1. **City buses**

2. **Trains or rails**

   • Understand the ticket machines. If traveling abroad, most automated ticket machines will be in the country's native language. Many major train stations have employees to help you navigate the machines. But count on your own notes and maps.

- Purchase tickets a month before your travel set date. Sometimes, the fare may be less expensive if you purchase your tickets well in advance.

- Determine the cost and if the machines accept credit cards or currency, especially if purchasing at a kiosk or a machine in a station. Ask the hotel concierge where, how, and when to purchase a ticket to the airport.

- **Very important!** Ask hotel CS or the train personnel what time the trains stop running through the station at night. Stations outside of major cities might stop running until the morning or following week.

3. **Taxis**

4. **Shuttle Services**

- Know the pick-up spots.

- Is there a set charge from the hotel to the airport?

- Can you prepay?

- Which service is the most reliable and safe?

- Always carry a 100 count of currency so you can give the precise amount plus a tip.

- Look up the driver's name or badge with the transportation company.

5. **UBER or OTHER professional transport companies (similar services, limousines, or hotel shuttles)**

- Make sure your GPS location is correct.

- Find a safe pickup location.

- Match the driver's ID from the app with the driver's description upon arrival—BEFORE entering the vehicle!

- Ask for a photo ID before entering the vehicle (if you are uncomfortable).

- Set aside currency for a tip.

- If possible, make sure the drop-off site is in a public, well-traveled area.

Throughout Europe, they use another source of transportation called BlaBlaCar, an ingenious platform created as a long-distance carpooling program. According to their website:

BlaBlaCar is the world's leading long-distance carpooling platform—a global, trusted community of eighty million drivers and passengers in twenty-two countries. The platform connects people looking to travel long distances with drivers heading the same way, so they can travel together and share the cost. With the recent integration of a

*coach network and a commuter carpooling service,
BlaBlaCar aims to become the go-to marketplace
for shared road mobility.*

OUR KEY NUMBERS:
Eighty million members in twenty-two countries
©2019 BlaBlaCar www.blablacar.com

Europe and other countries around the world also offer shrink-wrap machines that can wrap your luggage. If you are afraid that your articles (underwear) will fly out onto the airport turnstile or if the zipper on your luggage is broken, try this out.

I often take a trip to the airport the day before to get my bearings straight. I locate the area in the airport where my plane will depart from, the restrooms, and the CS agents specific to my airline. This bit of advice is important. It alleviates tracking down someone who can speak your language at the last moment or being led down an endless path of CS agents who don't know how to best assist you.

Get a lot of rest and eat a good meal before proceeding to the airport. Anticipate long lines with other travelers, mistaken service stations, repackaging your luggage—or anything that's unexpected! This is not to frighten you, but to inform you that life will sometimes throw a wrench into your plans. Rest up!

MY EXPERIENCE

As I booked my flights into London, I decided to try a different airport for flying out to Madrid after my stay there. I chose Gatwick Airport. If I had done my research at home, I would have known that Gatwick is roughly one HOUR away from central London! The day before I left, I checked for transportation. That is when I found out the distance and the time I would need to wake up to catch my Madrid flight.

Let's just say the taxi ride was very expensive.

Please don't repeat my mistake—unless you like getting up really early in the morning for one-hour drives in unfamiliar vehicles!

CHECKLIST

✓ Plan the distance and time and transportation to the airport. Use your map for travel between the airport and the hotel (or wherever to choose to stay).

✓ Put a visit to the major airport a day before your scheduled flight on your calendar to alleviate confusion on the day of the flight.

✓ Anticipate needing rest and a good meal the day before your flight.

✓ Find the easiest transportation option that will take you directly to the airport. Ask a concierge or the CS agent you booked with for advice.

TOOLKIT

✓ Properly labeled luggage with your home address, all landing zones, and your final destination if you need connecting flights.

✓ Use an identifying marker on your luggage (a colored ribbon, luggage belt, or address tag). This will not only help in identifying it among thousands of pieces of luggage in baggage claim. This will not only help you identify it in baggage claim, it will also aid you if your luggage is delayed and you need to provide a description to airline CS agents.

RESOURCES

✓ Use the airport's website to locate available transportation options directly to your residence from the airport.

*Beautiful antique fixtures, antique tiles and antique furniture are
sometimes the highlight of selecting a place of residency. However,
antique water lines that don't flush properly because they are the
same lines from the 17th century are not as exciting!*

Residency Preferences—
Comfort, Value, and
Member Services

ALTHOUGH THE LISTING SHOWS mostly hotel preferences, you can match the information below to motels, bed and breakfasts, hostels, cabins, rented condos, apartments, or houses.

Preferences are based on amenities and specific locations that accommodate the individual. Several selections are listed below.

* Bed sizes and the comfort of the bed
* The style of the rooms
* Bathroom toiletries, robes, and a shower vs. a tub
* Kitchens (stoves, microwaves, refrigerators, tea or coffee makers, and utensils)
* Self-serve laundromats or pick-up services from cleaners
* Balconies
* Panoramic views
* Safes for valuables
* Proximity to airports, downtown, and restaurants, wineries, or breweries
* Airport shuttles
* Pools, hot tubs, saunas, and workout rooms
* Daily cleaning by staff
* Gender or adult-specific considerations

* Lower fares included with airline reservations
* Boutiques (family-owned or bed and breakfasts)
* National chains (member exclusive deals and points)
* Provided breakfast
* Restaurant on-premises
* AAA travel promotions
* Updated rooms and foyers
* Safe neighborhoods for walking
* Vicinity to train, rail, or bus terminals
* Workout facilities
* Great or good CS

Clean and comfortable beds and updated rooms are my first priority.

According to an article by Rachel Sylvester in the July 12, 2019 edition of "Martha Stewart-Real Simple," there are preferable days to check-in during the week for economical purposes and to obtain the best room. Options include:

* Checking into the hotel on a Sunday.
* Booking the hotel one to two weeks in advance.
* Calling the specific hotel (not the national chain) directly.

CHECKLIST

✓ Categorize in three columns what you
would prefer regarding hotels, motels, bed
and breakfasts, and hostels.

✓ Have your map available to plan travel
to and from the airport, to the downtown
area, to entertainment, and more.

✓ Attend a one- or two-day course given by
a tour group, cruise agency, or featured
speaker. Being a member of AAA is essential for me because I get twenty-four-hour
mobile phone care when I travel, extensive
and exclusive deals (only for members),
travel printed guides for all parts of the
world for purchase at their agency, in-house
travel agents to book all types of travel—
local or overseas, and different types of
world currencies to purchase.

RESOURCES

✓ Choose a travel agency such as AAA or
  a local agency, or use a search engine to
  purchase these items.

✓ Look up specific hotel brands, bed and
  breakfasts, hostels, or residency apps,
  websites, or third-party search engines like
  Travelocity, Hotels.com, or TripAdvisor.

✓ Research websites such as TripAdvisor.
  com, lonelyplanet.com, Airbnb magazine,
  condenast.com, and popular travel blogs
  that rank hotels, Airbnbs, and hostels that
  interest you.

Aboard a cruise ship that sailed to Puerto Rico, a Bahama island owned exclusively by the cruise line, and the U.S. Virgin Islands. The specialty of the vacationing on a cruise ship is enjoying their planned activities such as the "Captains Dinner", variety of Entertainment options and grouping together with other like-minded tourists.

Cruises or Extended Train Excursions

CRUISE OR EXTENDED train excursions are compatible vacation options. First, they offer transportation, meal options at different intervals, single accommodations, automatic entertainment (set up by the ship or train), professional security, and gifts and convenience items. You can visit other countries or islands with other fellow travelers on the same transportation vehicle. There are many benefits, so this may be a starting point for your first solo vacation. They build awareness about what to expect when traveling to other countries, islands, and territories.

If you select a cruise ship as your option, bring along a formal outfit for what they call the Captains Dinner. It is an elegant evening with exquisite food selections and entertainment.

This vacation option is exceptional for the first time solo traveler.

(Helpful information may be referenced in the HOTEL section of this guidebook.)

CHECKLIST

✓ Look up which items can or cannot be brought on board.

✓ Budget in the cost of the flight and transportation along with your accommodations on the vessel of your choice.

✓ Bring a formal dinner outfit if you are traveling on a cruise ship.

✓ Bring your passport with you when docking at a port or stopping at a train station for the night.

✓ Make sure your airline flight arrival coordinates with the launching of the cruise ship from its home port. Allow at least six hours of leeway before the cruise ship departs, in case of flight delays or cancellations.

RESOURCES

✓ Use a reputable service when booking your travel: AAA, a local travel agency, a third-party website, or an exclusive site dedicated to cruise lines or train expeditions.

*Ole'! I've never seen a bullring before.
Don't worry. It was only a museum!*

Entertainment Venues:
Time vs. Safety

FULFILLING YOUR LIFELONG dream of visiting a country invigorates the soul! Whether you see a flamenco show in Spain, Notre Dame in Paris, the symphony in Vienna, find the best pho in Vietnam, or trek up to the highest point on the Great Wall of China, GO SEE IT!

Here are some things to consider before you head out of the door pertaining to your entertainment venues:

★ Time vs. safety.
★ Do you need to travel across the city?
★ Will you need a taxi?
★ How many trains or taxis would you need to get to the destination?
★ Does the venue include dinner?
★ What are the demographics? More children or men? Couples or tourists?
★ Can you purchase tickets in advance?
★ Can you find discounts or coupons associated with the location?
★ Where do you pick up the tickets: at the hotel, the location, or online?
★ Can you tag along with a tour group?

CHECKLIST

✓ Research entertainment options in a city or a nearby city that interest you.

✓ Use your map to travel between your residence and entertainment options.

✓ Research when you will leave the venue and related transportation options.

✓ Look for satisfying tours during the day.

✓ Research discounts or coupons associated with the venue and where you can pick up the tickets or if you can order online.

✓ Collect brochures and hotel maps for your entertainment options that list discounts and restaurants within the area.

✓ Find out the best route and transportation options to the vicinity.

✓ Purchase tickets ahead of time.

RESOURCES

✓ Download entertainment information from travel sites like AAA, TripAdvisor, Entertainment-Plus.net (North America only), and Viator.com.

✓ Select the places you'll visit on the maps and underline them, tab the entries, or call CS for more information.

Traveling is a fun adventure to undertake. However, safety and adhering to rules and warnings posted by the U.S. Department of State website on the countries you visit is a great idea.

Safety

WHETHER TRAVELING SOLO or with a group, safety always resides with the individual. We must always be aware of the items we pack, the transportation we schedule, and the surroundings of our walks. Several tips are mentioned below. However, I sprinkled wisdom throughout this guide.

MY EXPERIENCE

I traveled to Madrid, Spain, with my husband and my two sons (who were ten and twelve years old at the time). One day, in the deep heat of August, we took the hop on/ hop off bus tour of the downtown section of Madrid. My husband decided to extend his time with my oldest son. My youngest son and I decided to make our way back to the hotel. I shrugged off verifying with my husband the exact location, thinking I had memorized the hotel and the train stop. When we got to the train station, I couldn't remember the stop for our hotel. Believing I knew the direction from the train map, we headed off.

The only thing I remembered well was that our hotel was located near a popular shopping mall. I saw the name of the mall, El Corte Ingles, from the train, so we got off at the station.

BIG MISTAKE! Almost every mall in Spain, including several malls in Madrid, uses that same name! We wondered throughout, asking questions in broken Spanish, and we hopped onto other trains to the other identical malls with the same name. We finally found a hotel with an attendant who spoke English. She spoke with a taxi driver and gave him the address of our hotel. We arrived five hours later, finding my husband in a state of panic!

Learn from my mistake. I did!

* Use a map with a one or two block radius of the vicinity when booking a hotel.
* Carry your passport, a business card from your residence, your medical information, your cell phone, and enough currency at all times to aid you in difficult circumstances.

* Make sure your cell phone has data reception in advance (phone calls, text, and GPS guidance).
* Bring a water bottle and gum or candy.
* Use a portable charger adapter.
* Carry a day's worth of medication with you.
* Write down the local taxi company's phone number.
* Know the police and embassy phone numbers and addresses.
* Buy a translation pocketbook for the country's language.
* Be aware of your alcohol consumption.
* Make sure your purse and cell phone are with you at ALL times.
* Never leave your food or drink alone when you need to step away. Finish your drink. When you come back to the bar or table, ask for a clean glass.
* Watch the bartender pour your drink.
* When leaving an establishment at night, text a friend or loved one the driver's name, license plate, and the make of the car.

All of this information is for your benefit. It may seem self-explanatory, but I care about all my readers, so I must present it to you!

CHECKLIST

✓ Research the vicinity of your residence (hotels, bed and breakfasts, or hostels).

✓ Research transportation options around the location and time of your departure and arrival.

✓ Keep your identification, purse, and valuables with you at all times.

✓ Do you remember how to get back to your residence? Is the train or bus still running? Can you catch a taxi from your location?

✓ If you take a selfie stick, remember it is the destination, not the obstacle! Use discretion around cliffs, bodies of water, animals, and high-traffic areas.

TOOLKIT

✓ Enough currency (in 100 or 200 increments) to stay an additional night at your residence.

✓ Carry the business card of the residency location where you are staying. The card must display the name, CS agent (if possible), and the address and phone number, as well as the name of a CS agent.

✓ Your cell phone (of course) and a portable cell phone charger.

✓ Your water bottle, candy, gum, or energy bars to provide glucose for stamina and hydration.

✓ A packet of tissues.

RESOURCES

✓ There are several digital breathalyzers on the market that connect to your cell phone or its own device, including BACtrack, Aoxin, AlcoMate, and AlcoHAWK.

✓ View listings and ratings at www.bestreviews.com/best-breathalyzers.

RESOURCES

✓ Use a reputable service when booking your travel: AAA, a local travel agency, a third-party website, or an exclusive site dedicated to cruise lines or train expeditions.

Taking time to walk along a beach in Wintler Park, Vancouver, Washington. Walking is very beneficial for the mind, body and soul. Enjoy whatever environment you choose to take in the views and the scenery

Health

MAINTAINING YOUR HEALTH and medical references is critical. Check them before booking your flights or trains. Examine your health insurance plan to find out what your coverage is (i.e., doctor's visits, emergency rooms, and medications). Many countries will not proceed with medical care unless they first get payment in advance. AAA or other related travel agencies include these options in their plans, in case of emergency. Check with a travel consultant, health care provider, or insurance CS agent before signing the dotted line.

WAYS TO STAY HEALTHY BEFORE AND DURING YOUR TRIP

* Drink bottled water from a trusted company.

* Bring an empty water container for quick fill-ups.

* Check your current immunizations and fulfill the gaps!

* Carry a current medication list with daily doses and the contact information for the medical provider who issued the prescriptions.

* Purchase vitamin C, antacids, stool softeners, mints, cough drops, pain relievers, HAND SANITIZER, disinfectant sprays for bathroom breaks, tissues, bandages, eye drops, elastic wrap bandages for sprains, and earplugs before your trip.

* Pack an extra pair of glasses or contacts.

* Consume candy for low blood sugar.

* Eat low-carbohydrate, low-meat, and low-spice foods before bedtime.

* Try to eat three hours before bedtime.

* Drink seltzer, ginger ale, or a non-caffeinated soda for stomach upsets.

* Keep the caffeinated drinks to a minimum for proper sleep.

* Alcoholic drinks are nice for a nightcap, but know your limitations and the distortions they can instill.

* Place a photograph of your family and friends near your bed.

* Read a book to soothe your soul and quiet you for a good night's sleep.

* Pack portable slip-ons in case of shoe breakage.

Your scheduled itinerary does not dictate your trip. You design it every morning you wake up! Whether you want to explore the hotel's surroundings on foot, read that book that you squished into the back of your luggage, watch different programs shown on the television that you can't watch in America, or take that extra, invigorating snooze—you've arrived! You've fulfilled the most stressful part of traveling. Now enjoy!

CHECKLIST

✓ Check your health insurance plan.

✓ Bring paperwork from your pharmacy or doctor regarding your prescriptions.

✓ Stock up on health essentials, but remember there are pharmacies and convenience stores that carry the same brands.

✓ Keep eating to a minimum before bedtime. Indigestion is not a good sleeping agent, and most pharmacies will be closed during the night. If you must enjoy that dinner, purchase a soda from the vending machine to aid your possible stomach issues.

✓ Being well hydrated is a must!

✓ Monitor eating, alcohol, and caffeinated drinks.

RESOURCES

✓ Download your health insurance app,
   which provides essential information such
   as your current prescription list, doctor's
   name, surgeries, medical information,
   allergy list, and much more detailed
   information.

✓ Use Diabetes Forecast, AARP, FITNESS,
   or any other app that can provide healthy
   food options for you as you travel.

✓ Purchase a step counter app such as FITBIT,
   Step Counter on Google Play, Nike Fuel-
   Band, Apple Health App, or any other
   pedometer app.

*A day bag or backpack is essential as you will probably
be on foot all day or you will want to purchase souvenirs.
Stop looking at the statue!*

Packing

MOST AREAS IN THE WORLD will have sunscreen, hats, hand sanitizer, umbrellas, swimsuits (just in case), pain relievers, socks, flip-flops, and other comforts. I advise you to buy tampons or large panty liners or pads before leaving home. International companies sell different feminine hygiene items, and the hotel or mini-mart across from your hotel may not fit your specific sizes or needs. Also, buy wet wipes for hygiene purposes or bring a small three-ounce spray bottle of disinfectant (Lysol comes to mind) wherever you travel.

A well-seasoned traveler offered me sage wisdom on an item that should always be packed somewhere with your luggage: Tupperware, luncheon sandwich bags, or a foldable meal container. You may need to warm up your dinner leftovers the next day or carry them to your next journey.

Bring travel-size laundry detergent for small loads on the go. You can purchase these from your local convenience store or laundromat. Do NOT pack detergent in sandwich bags or other containers. I recommend original packaging, in case of airport security checks. Preferably, purchase the powder version in case of a puncture in the packet.

WASHING CLOTHES

Rule: DO NOT wash clothes in the evening if you plan to wear them the next day, especially if the item is made of cotton such as jeans or coats! Attempt this procedure with different types of clothing (underwear!) at home before you leave for your trip. Underwear will sometimes dry overnight. But if you travel to a humid climate, it may take more time to dry.

I encourage packing lighter by washing your clothes multiple times during your trip. This puts less weight on your suitcase and causes less pain when heaving it up onto luggage racks, stairs, or airplane compartments. Also, many items can be interchangeable.

Several cathedrals do not allow shorts. Pants or skirts below the knee are acceptable. In some countries you may visit, a handy shawl or scarf may be needed to cover your head.

A good train of thought: this is their country (if traveling abroad), and showing respect is highly advisable. Other woman travelers will follow after you. Please leave a good impression.

Bring along your own headphones or AirPods. It is convenient and resourceful as you travel in airplanes and whatever transportation you use, and your personal headphones are more sanitary than the complimentary package of headphones found every-where. From airlines, trains, or even the hop on/hop off tour buses, I wouldn't take a chance on recycled headphones!

Remember, whatever you bring, consider the weight, size, and bag you will carry to a destination. You can easily take a high-definition picture with the newest cell phone out on the market. Binoculars called Snapzooms allow you to take pictures through their device. Companies offer several tripod adapters for every cell phone, charging stations, and fast chargers as emergency backup power sources when you aren't near an electrical socket. Think three times before you bring your Canon, Nikon, or another professional photography camera.

Very important! Try very hard to pack only a twenty-two-inch piece of luggage and your purse, backpack, or fanny pack. I know it may sound unbearable. You will probably need to put your luggage above your airline or train seat and move at an incredible speed, as other people will be waiting to get to their seats. Many train stations or bus locations don't have escalators or elevators. You will, most definitely, lug your belongings up a flight of stairs, rush into a train before it leaves, or heave it into a taxicab trunk. AND... you will need to walk to your hotel or other residence, which may be a block or more away. Please give this some serious consideration.

CHECKLIST

✓ Pack light! Bring interchangeable clothing.

✓ Start packing a week to a week and a half before your home departure date. This will enable you to rethink if you need that extra item or not. Revisit your luggage several times during the week.

✓ Do not bring large personal items such as toothpaste, deodorant, and shampoo unless you are going camping for a week or trekking across a desert or hiking Kilimanjaro. Purchase the three-ounce versions (permissible at all airports) for convenience.

✓ Do not handwash cotton or items that take longer to air dry.

TOOLKIT

✓ Hand sanitizer and feminine hygiene items from your home location that are personal and suited to you.

✓ Powdered laundry detergent in its own box.

✓ A selfie stick.

- ✓ Your own headphones or AirPods.

- ✓ A handy shawl or scarf.

- ✓ Neck pillow and earplugs (or your headset or headphones) for a peaceful sleep on transportation.

- ✓ Very important! A portable phone charger for instant cell phone charging while you are on the go.

- ✓ All cell phone portable chargers, portable devices, and selfie stick chargers.

- ✓ Small snacks to boost your sugar or energy levels (gum, hard candy, or energy bars).

- ✓ Very important! An empty water bottle for constant hydration.

- ✓ Pharmacy notes for medications and eyeglass prescriptions.

*Visiting St. Michael's Church in Hamburg, Germany.
This place is where I found solace and peace, after a
long plane flight and a taxi ride.*

Conclusion

IN CONCLUSION, your trip will be fine as long as you research the topics I have included in this handbook and the advice of others who have traveled solo, with a tour group, or with family and friends.

Remember this quote: if life gives you lemons, make lemonade!

If you miss your train during your vacation, another one will come, or the concierge will share trustworthy information.

Bring enough currency in case you need a taxicab, your cell phone (charged), a language book from the country you are visiting, a few bathroom essentials (in case you can't return to your original residence and need another place to stay), and a small notebook. You can also type any identifiable road markers into your NOTES app or retrace some visible clues to get you back to your residency. HOWEVER, I advise you to be alert and cognizant of your whereabouts, and bring your essentials with you at all times.

In respect to circumstances occurring during travel that may be beyond your control, there will be people of trust to turn to. An embassy, bank, police station, pharmacy, cathedral or church, hotel or hostel CS, or other reputable CS representative may offer recommendations in sticky situations.

You must be clear-minded, calm, and know your surroundings (north, south, east, and west) at all times. Find various transportation options in case you need to stay at a nearby hotel or other location for the night. This will enable you to rest and gather your thoughts logically.

I can only offer my suggestions from my thirty-five years of experience, traveling three to four times a year with or without companions. Let's just say I carry an inquisitive, overly cautious, determined, and optimistic resilience with me—a will is what it is called. This handbook merely reflects it. A handbook is a guide for traveling, not an absolute that replaces your own decision-making.

Please take this handbook or tear out certain pages for reference. Fit or squeeze them into your luggage, day organizer, or bag, or fold them into your pocket. Write notes, and use them for a scribble pad or everything else you can think of. I'm good with that!

Acknowledgments

Thank you to all who were involved with the whole process!

My GOD

George Vigil

Joshua Vigil

Gabriel Vigil

Polly Letofsky

Jen Zellinger

Victoria Wolf

and all those women over the years, who said to me, "I couldn't do that."